CONNECT BIBLE STUDIES

Computer Animated Films

Toy Story & Toy Story 2
Finding Nemo
Monsters, Inc.
Shrek & Shrek 2

www.connectbiblestudies.com

connect
linking the Word to the world

CONNECT BIBLE STUDIES: Computer Animated Films

Published in this format by Scripture Union, 207–209 Queensway, Bletchley, MK2 2EB, England.
Scripture Union is an international Christian charity working with churches in more than 130 countries providing resources to bring the good news about Jesus Christ to children, young people and families – and to encourage them to develop spiritually through the Bible and prayer. As well as a network of volunteers, staff and associates who run holidays, church-based events and school Christian groups, Scripture Union produces a wide range of publications and supports those who use the resources through training programmes.
Email: info@scriptureunion.org.uk
Internet: www.scriptureunion.org.uk

© Damaris Trust, PO Box 200, Southampton, SO17 2DL
Damaris Trust enables people to relate Christian faith and contemporary culture. It helps them to think about issues within society from a Christian perspective and explore God's truth as it is revealed in the Bible. Damaris provides resources via the Internet, workshops, publications and products.
Email: office@damaris.org
Internet: www.damaris.org

British Library Cataloguing-in-Publication Data: a catalogue record for this book is available from the British Library.
First published 2004 ISBN 1 84427 115 3

ALSO AVAILABLE AS AN ELECTRONIC DOWNLOAD: www.connectbiblestudies.com

Damaris writers: Di Archer, Caroline Puntis, Peter S Williams
SU editors: Andrew Cupples, Andrew Clark

Cover design by Aricot Vert of Fleet, UK.

Cover photo © PDI/Dreamworks. Used with permission.

Print production by CPO, Garcia Estate, Canterbury Road, Worthing, West Sussex, BN13 1BW.
CPO is a Christian publishing charity working in partnership with over 30,000 churches and other Christian organisations worldwide, using the power of design and print to convey the message of Jesus Christ. Established for over 45 years, CPO is the UK's premier supplier of publicity and related resources to the UK Church, available through a direct mail catalogue series, an e-commerce website and most Christian bookshops.
Email: connect@cpo.org.uk
Internet: www.cpo-online.org

Other titles in this series:

Harry Potter 1 85999 578 0	**TV Game Shows** 1 85999 609 4
Destiny's Child: *Survivor* 1 85999 613 2	**Lord of the Rings** 1 85999 634 5
The Simpsons 1 85999 529 2	**Dido:** *No Angel* 1 85999 679 5
Sven: *On Football* 1 85999 690 6	**Pullman:** *His Dark Materials* 1 85999 714 7
Friends 1 85999 775 9	**Madonna** 1 84427 032 7
James Bond 1 84427 007 6	**John Grisham's Thrillers** 1 84427 021 1
The Matrix Trilogy 1 84427 061 0	**TV Soaps** 1 84427 087 4

Titles available as electronic download only:
U2: *All That You Can't Leave Behind*/ **Billy Elliot**/ **Chocolat**/ **How to be Good**/ **AI: Artificial Intelligence**/ **Iris**/ **Superheroes**
And more titles following. Check www.connectbiblestudies.com for latest titles or ask at any good Christian bookshop.

linking the Word to the world

Using Connect Bible Studies

What Are These Studies?

These innovative home group Bible studies have two aims. Firstly, to enable group members to dig into their Bibles and get to know them better. Secondly, by being based on contemporary films, books, TV programmes, music, etc., the aim is to help people think through topical issues in a biblical way.

It is not envisaged that all members will always be able to watch the films, play the music or read the books, or indeed that they will always want to. A summary is always provided. However, our vision is that knowing about these films and books empowers Christians to engage with friends and colleagues about them. Addressing issues from a biblical perspective gives Christians confidence that they know what they think, and can bring a distinctive angle to bear in conversations.

The studies are produced in sets of four – ie four weeks' worth of group Bible Study material. These are available in print published by Scripture Union from your local Christian bookshop, or via the Internet: www.connectbiblestudies.com. Anyone can sign up for a free monthly email newsletter that announces the new studies and provides other information (click on 'sign up' at www.connectbiblestudies.com).

How Do I Use Them?

These studies are designed to stimulate creative thought and discussion within a biblical context. Each section therefore has a range of questions or options from which you as leader may choose in order to tailor the study to your group's needs and desires. Different approaches may appeal at different times, so the studies aim to supply lots of choice. Whilst adhering to the main aim of corporate Bible study, some types of questions may enable this for your group better than others – so take your pick.

Group members should be supplied with the appropriate sheet that they can fill in, each one also showing the relevant summary.

Leader's notes contain:

1 Opening questions

These help your group settle in to discussion, while introducing the topics. They may be straightforward, personal or creative, but aim to provoke a response.

2 Summary

We suggest the summary of the book or film will follow now, read aloud if necessary. There may well be reactions that group members want to express even before getting on to the week's issue.

3 Key issue

Again, either read from the leader's notes, or summarise.

4 Bible study

Lots of choice here. Choose as appropriate to suit your group – get digging into the Bible. Background reading and texts for further help and study are suggested, but please use the material provided to inspire your group to explore their Bibles as much as possible. A concordance might be a handy standby for looking things up. A commentary could be useful too, such as the New Bible Commentary 21st century edition (IVP, 1994). The idea is to help people to engage with the truth of God's word, wrestling with it if necessary but making it their own.

Don't plan to work through every question here. Within each section the two questions explore roughly the same ground but from different angles or in different ways. Our advice is to take one question from each section. The questions are open-ended so each ought to yield good discussion – though of course any discussion in a Bible study may need prompting to go a little further.

5 Implications

Here the aim is to tie together the perspectives gained through Bible study and the impact of the book or film. The implications may be personal, a change in worldview, or new ideas for relating to non-churchgoers. Choose questions that adapt to the flow of the discussion.

6 Prayer

Leave time for it! We suggest a time of open prayer, or praying in pairs if the group would prefer. Encourage your members to focus on issues from your study that had a particular impact on them. Try different approaches to prayer – light a candle, say a prayer each, write prayers down, play quiet worship music – aiming to facilitate everyone to relate to God.

7 Background reading

You will find links to some background reading on the Connect Bible Studies website: www.connectbiblestudies.com

8 Online Discussion

You can discuss the studies online with others at www.damaris.org/discuss/

www.connectbiblestudies.com

connect
linking the Word to the world

Toy Story & Toy Story 2

Disney/Pixar

Computer Animated Films: Part One

Woody: [Chairing the toys' staff meeting.] **Hey listen, no one's getting replaced. This is Andy we're talking about. It doesn't matter how much we're played with. What matters is that we're here for Andy when he needs us. That's what we're here for, right?** (*Toy Story*)

Please read Using Connect Bible Studies *(page 3) before leading a Bible study with this material.*

Opening Questions

Choose one of these questions.

Which is your favourite *Toy Story* movie and why?	Which toy from the *Toy Story* films would you like to own and why?
What was your favourite toy as a child? Describe what it meant to you.	Do children have too many toys these days? Why/why not?

Summary

Little does Andy know that once he is out of his bedroom, his toys come alive. Although Andy loves and cares for his toys, they live under a shadow – if he stops playing with them, they could end up in the next yard sale. Life is particularly turbulent around birthdays and Christmas time, when exciting new toys arrive on the scene.

Enter the multi-talented Buzz Lightyear, a Space Ranger toy who genuinely believes he is on a mission to save the planet. The previous favourite, Woody the cowboy, is ousted from pride of place on Andy's bed by this new rival. Determined to find his way back to Andy's heart, Woody seizes an opportunity to get rid of Buzz – with disastrous consequences. The two toys end up with next door's child Sid, a toy-destroyer. As Buzz realises that he is only a toy, Woody helps him to find his true value and purpose – in belonging to Andy. Together, they find a way to get home.

The themes are picked up in *Toy Story 2*. When Woody is kidnapped by a collector of rare toys, he discovers that he is valuable memorabilia from an old TV show. It looks like Buzz and friends have come to the rescue too late – Woody has been persuaded that it would be better to live forever in a box than to be thrown away in a yard sale. It is only when he rubs away the newly-applied paint from the sole of his shoe to reveal Andy's name that he understands where his future really lies.

Key Issue: The imagination of *Toy Story* and *Toy Story 2*

Toy Story captured the imagination of millions and was a box office smash; many thought that *Toy Story 2* was even better. As well as breaking new ground with their computer animated graphics, the creators of Woody and friends had two noteworthy hits to their credit. But it wasn't just the way it was done that made them so successful – it was the stories too. So we look at what the Bible has to say about the amazing imagination displayed in these films, and the recognisable themes of belonging, rivalry and the courage the toys have to find in order to be faithful to each other. We have all been in these difficult situations, but have we handled them as well as these animated toys?

Bible Study

Choose one question from each section.

1   Imagination

Woody: ***Why would Andy want you? Look at you – you're a Buzz Lightyear! Any other toy would give up his moving parts just to be you. You've got wings! You glow in the dark! You talk! Your helmet does that . . . whoosh thing! You are a cool toy.***
(*Toy Story*)

◆   Read Job 40:15–24. How does this description of the behemoth capture your imagination? What is the relationship between Creator and created?

Leaders: These verses are part of God's reply to Job's challenge that he had wronged him. The creature is real rather than mythical, usually identified with the hippopotamus.

◆   Read Revelation 4:1–11. How does this imagery impact you emotionally? What do the pictures in your head tell you about God?

2   Belonging

Buzz Lightyear: ***Life's only worth living if you're being loved by a kid.*** (*Toy Story 2*)

◆   Read Jeremiah 31:31–40. What is the purpose of the new covenant God will make with Israel? In what ways do God's people belong to him?

◆   Read Romans 8:9–17. How do we belong to Christ? What are the consequences?

3   Rivalry

Mr. Potato Head: ***Couldn't handle Buzz cutting in on your play time, could you Woody? Didn't want to face the fact that Buzz just might be Andy's new favourite toy, so you got rid of him. Well, what if Andy starts playing with me more, Woody, huh? You gonna knock me out of the window too?*** (*Toy Story*)

◆   Read 1 Samuel 18:1–16. What did Saul's jealousy do to him? What did Saul's jealousy do to David?

Leaders: You may wish to follow Saul and David's story in section 4 also.

◆   Read Mark 9:33–37; 10:35–45. What did the disciples' rivalry do to their relationships? How does Jesus challenge what they long for?

4   Courage to be faithful

Buzz Lightyear: ***Woody once risked his life to save me. I couldn't call myself his friend if I weren't willing to do the same.*** (*Toy Story 2*)

◆   Read 1 Samuel 20:1–17. Why did Jonathan lose faith in Saul? What motivated Jonathan to protect David?

◆   Read Acts 4:1–22. What motivated Peter to stand up for Jesus? What impact did Peter and John's faith have on the different people in this situation?

Implications

Woody: ***Being a toy is a lot better than being a Space Ranger ... Look, over in that house is a kid who thinks you are the greatest. And it's not because you're a Space Ranger, pal. It's because you're a toy. You are his toy.*** (*Toy Story*)

Choose one or more of the following questions.

◆   How does God speak to you through his creativity? How do you express your creativity?

◆   Christians have sometimes been wary of using imagination. When is it helpful to you and are there times when it is not?

◆   How would you describe to a non-believer what it means for you to belong to Christ?

◆   What difference does belonging to God make to your life? Are there ways in which it could make more of a difference?

◆   What situations arouse jealousy in you? How could God's perspective help you?

◆   How do you handle situations of conflicting loyalties?

◆   When do you find it hardest to stand up for Jesus? How can God, and your group, help you in this?

◆   Have you ever used toys to communicate God's story? How?

Prayer

Spend some time praying through these issues.

Background Reading

You will find links to some background reading on the Connect Bible Studies website: www.connectbiblestudies.com

Discuss

Discuss this study in the online discussion forums at www.damaris.org/discuss/

Members' Sheet – *Toy Story & Toy Story 2*

Summary

Little does Andy know that once he is out of his bedroom, his toys come alive. Although Andy loves and cares for his toys, they live under a shadow – if he stops playing with them, they could end up in the next yard sale. Life is particularly turbulent around birthdays and Christmas time, when exciting new toys arrive on the scene.

Enter the multi-talented Buzz Lightyear, a Space Ranger toy who genuinely believes he is on a mission to save the planet. The previous favourite, Woody the cowboy, is ousted from pride of place on Andy's bed by this new rival. Determined to find his way back to Andy's heart, Woody seizes an opportunity to get rid of Buzz – with disastrous consequences. The two toys end up with next door's child Sid, a toy-destroyer. As Buzz realises that he is only a toy, Woody helps him to find his true value and purpose – in belonging to Andy. Together, they find a way to get home.

The themes are picked up in *Toy Story 2*. When Woody is kidnapped by a collector of rare toys, he discovers that he is valuable memorabilia from an old TV show. It looks like Buzz and friends have come to the rescue too late – Woody has been persuaded that it would be better to live forever in a box than to be thrown away in a yard sale. It is only when he rubs away the newly-applied paint from the sole of his shoe to reveal Andy's name that he understands where his future really lies.

Key Issue

Bible Study notes

Implications

Prayer

Finding Nemo

Disney/Pixar

Computer Animated Films: Part Two

Nemo: **Dad, you're not going to freak out like you did at the petting zoo, are you?**

Marlin: **Hey, that snail was about to charge!**

Please read Using Connect Bible Studies *(page 3) before leading a Bible study with this material.*

Opening Questions

Choose one of these questions.

What do you like best about *Finding Nemo* and why?	If you were a character in *Finding Nemo*, which would you be and why?
Why are the fish in *Finding Nemo* so appealing?	Why do you think computer animated films are so popular?

Summary

The Great Barrier Reef is home to a happily married couple of clownfish, Marlin and Coral, and their children. Tragedy strikes this underwater community when a big fish with lots of teeth eats Coral and most of the kids. Only one son survives – Nemo, who has one fin smaller than the other. Terrified that he will lose Nemo too, Marlin becomes an over-protective father. Having let little Nemo attend school for the first time, Marlin suddenly decides that school trips are too dangerous and wants him to wait for another year. Ironically, Marlin's stifling approach to parenting leads young Nemo into a rebellious act – Nemo swims out towards a boat in deep water, gets caught by a scuba diver and ends up in a fish tank belonging to a Sydney dentist. Marlin loses no time. Determined to find his son, he sets off on an epic adventure from his coral reef home to the waters of Sydney harbour. On the way he hooks up with Dory, a happy-go-lucky fish who suffers from short-term memory loss.

Meanwhile, Nemo is doing his best to escape from the confines of his new tank before the dentist's nasty niece arrives to take him home with her. With some skill and a bit of luck, Nemo ends up finding his way back to the sea. He bumps into Dory who eventually remembers that Marlin was looking for his son Nemo, but has given up and gone home believing he is dead. She puts two and two together in the nick of time, and father and son are reunited. Once they are home, Marlin puts his new-found trust into practice and sends Nemo off to school.

Key Issue: Finding humanity in Nemo

Whether you usually find fish appealing or not, it would take a determined cynicism not to let Nemo win you round. The little fish with the big, brave heart leads us into the familiar waters of longing for independence, dealing with over-protective parents and struggling with an imperfect body. As the animated creatures with human characteristics face their big adventure on the screen, we are drawn into their story. So can the Bible help us with the tussle between child and parent, or living with our own limitations? What does it say about this powerful technique of using animals as an analogy for ourselves?

Bible Study

Choose one question from each section.

1   Creatures with human characteristics

Gill: ***You're lucky to have someone out there who's looking for you.***

◆   Read Psalm 91:1–4 and Habakkuk 1:5–15. Why do animals make good analogies in these passages?

Leaders: Habbakuk was struggling to understand why the wicked were going unpunished, and why God would choose the Babylonians to discipline Judah. In likening humans to animals, Psalm 91 and Habakkuk 1 stress both the earthly vulnerability and the eternal security offered by a relationship with God.

◆   Read Luke 15:1–7 and 1 Peter 2:25. What was Jesus suggesting about tax collectors and 'sinners'? What was he suggesting about the Pharisees and himself?

2 Living with imperfections

Marlin: *We call it his lucky fin.*

- Read Exodus 4:10–17. How did God see Moses' imperfection? What difference did this make to Moses?

- Read 2 Corinthians 12:1–10. How did God change Paul's attitude to his problems? Why does Paul like to boast about his weaknesses?

3 Breaking away from Dad

Marlin: *You know you can't swim well.*
Nemo: *I can swim fine, Dad, OK?*
Marlin: *No, it's not OK. You shouldn't be anywhere near here* (the edge of the reef). *OK, I was right. You'll start school in a year or two.*
Nemo: *No, Dad! Just because you're scared of the ocean.*
Marlin: *Clearly, you're not ready. And you're not coming back until you are. You think you can do these things but you just can't, Nemo!*
Nemo: *I hate you.*

Leaders: You may wish to follow the parable of the lost son in sections 3 and 4, especially if you read Luke 15:1–7 in section 1.

- Read Jonah 1:1–17. How did God deal with Jonah's rebellion? How were the sailors affected?

Leaders: See 2 Kings 14:25 and Matthew 12:38–41.

- Read Luke 15:11–32. What was at the heart of the younger son's desire to leave home? What did he learn about his father?

Leaders: Since a father's estate would normally be divided after his death, the younger son is in effect telling his father that he wished he were dead!

4 Letting go of your child

Marlin: [As Nemo goes off to school.] *Now go have an adventure!*

- Read Proverbs 4:1–27. What does the passage tell us about the relationships in this family? How did the father prepare his sons for leaving home?

- Read Luke 15:11–32. Why did the father divide up his estate and let his younger son leave home? How were the different relationships changed by this experience?

Leaders: See note with section 3.

Implications

Marlin: **I promised I'd never let anything happen to him.**

Dory: **Huh? That's a funny thing to promise! … you can't never let anything happen to him – then nothing would ever happen to him! Not much fun for little Harpo.**

Choose one or more of the following questions.

◆ Which *Finding Nemo* character best sums up your attitude to life? What effect does this have on your spiritual life?

◆ What are your expectations of how God will deal with your problems? Are they in line with what the Bible says?

◆ Which character in the parable of the lost son do you most identify with and why?

◆ How do you relate to God as Father? Do you assume he has characteristics which are not backed up by the Bible? How could you change this?

◆ Is breaking away from parents ever defensible? Why/why not? What about breaking away from God?

◆ Who do you look up to as being genuinely wise about life? What lessons could you learn from them?

◆ What is your attitude to your own imperfections? How do you think God wants you to see them?

◆ What would you say to someone who cannot see God as a caring father?

Prayer

Spend some time praying through these issues.

Background Reading

You will find links to some background reading on the Connect Bible Studies website: www.connectbiblestudies.com

Discuss

Discuss this study in the online discussion forums at www.damaris.org/discuss/

Members' Sheet – *Finding Nemo*

Summary

The Great Barrier Reef is home to a happily married couple of clownfish, Marlin and Coral, and their children. Tragedy strikes this underwater community when a big fish with lots of teeth eats Coral and most of the kids. Only one son survives – Nemo, who has one fin smaller than the other. Terrified that he will lose Nemo too, Marlin becomes an over-protective father. Having let little Nemo attend school for the first time, Marlin suddenly decides that school trips are too dangerous and wants him to wait for another year. Ironically, Marlin's stifling approach to parenting leads young Nemo into a rebellious act – Nemo swims out towards a boat in deep water, gets caught by a scuba diver and ends up in a fish tank belonging to a Sydney dentist. Marlin loses no time. Determined to find his son, he sets off on an epic adventure from his coral reef home to the waters of Sydney harbour. On the way he hooks up with Dory, a happy-go-lucky fish who suffers from short-term memory loss.

Meanwhile, Nemo is doing his best to escape from the confines of his new tank before the dentist's nasty niece arrives to take him home with her. With some skill and a bit of luck, Nemo ends up finding his way back to the sea. He bumps into Dory who eventually remembers that Marlin was looking for his son Nemo, but has given up and gone home believing he is dead. She puts two and two together in the nick of time, and father and son are reunited. Once they are home, Marlin puts his new-found trust into practice and sends Nemo off to school.

Key Issue

Bible Study notes

Implications

Prayer

www.connectbiblestudies.com

connect

linking the Word to the world

Monsters, Inc.

Disney/Pixar

Computer Animated Films: Part Three

Sulley: ***It might sound crazy, but I don't think that kid's dangerous.***

Please read Using Connect Bible Studies *(page 3) before leading a Bible study with this material.*

Opening Questions

Choose one of these questions.

Who is your favourite character in *Monsters, Inc.* and why?	Is *Monsters, Inc.* a scary film for children? Why/why not?
What were you scared of when you went to bed as a child?	Why do adults enjoy films like *Monsters, Inc.*?

Summary

Monsters, Inc. opens in Monstropolis, a happy place populated with implausibly-shaped monsters working, playing, eating and living. Sulley, a big, fluffy, blue bear of a monster, and his trainer Mike Wazowski, a one-eyed green sphere, set off to work. Mike is in love with receptionist Celia, and is behind on his paperwork, for which he is chastised by formidable snail Roz. The power for Monstropolis comes from children's screams, collected in yellow cannisters as the 'scarer' monsters go through children's closet doors to frighten them in their beds at night. But there is a twist: the monsters believe that children are toxic, and fling themselves into frightened decontamination routines if even a child's sock should enter their world.

Then, disaster, a little girl escapes into Monstropolis. The monsters panic, but Mike and Sulley uncover the truth that Boo – the child – is not dangerous, and decide to restore her to her world. Their arch-rival Randall wants to kidnap her for his scream-extractor, which will force screams out of children by machine. Much battling ensues between Randall and Sulley, until finally Randall is beaten and Mr Waternoose, the factory owner, is exposed as being involved in the kidnap plot. Roz turns up as an undercover agent, and Monstropolis discovers the truth about children. Sulley realises that children's laughs provide power too, so the monsters learn the art of comedy and dispense with their fear – and scaring. Mike enables Sulley to see Boo once again, to enjoy a friendship built on love not fear.

Key Issue: Monsters for all to love

Monsters who struggle with paperwork and are frightened of children; doors into another world and the cutest kid on the block; romance, tension and adventure – surely there is something for everyone in *Monsters, Inc.* As we consider the all-age appeal of animated films, represented by *Monsters, Inc.*, we also look at the big themes it introduces. There is lots of deception going on, and therefore plenty of fear. Thankfully, the truth eventually comes out. Back in the real world, where we get deceived and scared sometimes as well, what does the Bible say about the truth of our situation? Is God for all ages too?

Bible Study

Choose one question from each section.

1   For all ages

> *This is the kind of movie that works on multiple levels – as fast-moving, lively fun for children and as slyly written, visually impressive entertainment for adults.* (James Berardinelli, www.movie-reviews.colossus.net)

◆   Read 1 Samuel 3:1–21. How did God engage the attention of Eli in this story? What did the responses of both Eli and Samuel show about them?

◆   Read Mark 10:13–16. What did the children learn about Jesus? What did the adults learn about children?

2 Being deceived

Mr Waternoose: ***There's nothing more toxic or deadly than a human child. A single touch could kill you.***

Leaders: You may wish to continue with the Genesis passage in section 3 and the Titus questions in section 4.

◆ Read Genesis 3:1–7. How did the serpent manipulate Eve's understanding of God? Why did the reality of sin fail to deliver what Adam and Eve thought it would?

Leaders: Note that Adam is with Eve all the time here. Eve is willing to be tempted and gives in to temptation; her attempt to shift all the blame onto the serpent (Genesis 3:13) doesn't wash.

◆ Read Joshua 9:1–27. Why did the Gibeonite's ruse succeed? How did this deception affect the Israelites?

Leaders: Presumably the Gibeonites negatively influenced the Jews when it came to the issue of idolatry.

3 Fear

Trainee Scarer: ***I won't go in a kid's room. You can't make me!***

◆ Read Genesis 3:8–24. Why did Adam and Eve hide in the trees? How did fear drive Adam and Eve's response to God?

Leaders: Hiding in the trees, like the making of clothing (verse 7), symbolises the reluctance to be vulnerable and open before another that sin brings.

◆ Read Luke 8:22–25. Why did fear overwhelm the disciples' faith? Why didn't fear overwhelm Jesus?

Leaders: If the disciples' fear was the result of a lack of faith, their lack of faith was a result of their lack of understanding of who Jesus is (see the end of verse 25).

4 Truth

Mike: ***So now the truth comes out, doesn't it Sulley? What about everything we ever worked for, does that matter, huh? And what about me? I'm your pal, your best friend, don't I matter?***

◆ Read Titus 3:1–8. Why does living without God mean being deceived? How does living in the truth change us?

◆ Read John 3:1–21. Why is Jesus confident that he knows the truth? How does Jesus explain people's response to the truth?

Implications

> Mr Waternoose: **Times have changed. Scaring isn't enough ... I'll kidnap a thousand children before I let this company die and I'll silence anyone who gets in my way.**

Choose one or more of the following questions.

- In what ways is a relationship with God possible for a baby, a toddler, a child? How can you encourage children who you know?

- What do you need to learn from children in your relationship with God?

- What are you doing to ensure that you do not get deceived by the devil's lies, but are living in the truth?

- What doubts or struggles do you have with the truth Jesus brings? How can your group help you with them?

- What are you scared of? What can you do about this?

- How could your Christian community do more to ensure that all ages feel welcome?

- Why do we allow ourselves to be deceived?

- Do you hide from God, or others? What are you afraid of? What would encourage you to come into the open?

Prayer

Spend some time praying through these issues.

Background Reading

You will find links to some background reading on the Connect Bible Studies website: www.connectbiblestudies.com

Discuss

Discuss this study in the online discussion forums at www.damaris.org/discuss/

Members' Sheet – *Monsters, Inc.*

Summary

Monsters, Inc. opens in Monstropolis, a happy place populated with implausibly-shaped monsters working, playing, eating and living. Sulley, a big, fluffy, blue bear of a monster, and his trainer Mike Wazowski, a one-eyed green sphere, set off to work. Mike is in love with receptionist Celia, and is behind on his paperwork, for which he is chastised by formidable snail Roz. The power for Monstropolis comes from children's screams, collected in yellow cannisters as the 'scarer' monsters go through children's closet doors to frighten them in their beds at night. But there is a twist: the monsters believe that children are toxic, and fling themselves into frightened decontamination routines if even a child's sock should enter their world.

Then, disaster, a little girl escapes into Monstropolis. The monsters panic, but Mike and Sulley uncover the truth that Boo – the child – is not dangerous, and decide to restore her to her world. Their arch-rival Randall wants to kidnap her for his scream-extractor, which will force screams out of children by machine. Much battling ensues between Randall and Sulley, until finally Randall is beaten and Mr Waternoose, the factory owner, is exposed as being involved in the kidnap plot. Roz turns up as an undercover agent, and Monstropolis discovers the truth about children. Sulley realises that children's laughs provide power too, so the monsters learn the art of comedy and dispense with their fear – and scaring. Mike enables Sulley to see Boo once again, to enjoy a friendship built on love not fear.

Key Issue

Bible Study notes

Implications

Prayer

Shrek & Shrek 2

Dreamworks

Computer Animated Films: Part Four

Donkey: *Well, you know what I like about you, Shrek? You got that kind of I-don't-care-what-nobody-thinks-of-me thing. I like that. I respect that, Shrek. You all right.*

Please read Using Connect Bible Studies *(page 3) before leading a Bible study with this material.*

Opening Questions

Choose one of these questions.

What makes a fairy-tale ending, and do the *Shrek* films have them?	What is your favourite fairy tale and why?
Is Shrek ugly? Why/why not?	What is the funniest moment in either film and why?

Summary

Shrek is an ugly ogre who prefers a life of solitude to rejection. At the beginning of the film, he reads a fairy tale with sarcasm: 'Once upon a time there was a lovely princess ...' He has no time for fairy tales or fairy-tale creatures – until a talking donkey appears. Donkey is on the run from the evil Lord Farquaad, who has banished all fairy-tale creatures from his realm and designated Shrek's swamp as their new home. Furious at the disruption, Shrek sets off with Donkey to claim it back. He strikes a deal with Farquaad – he will rescue the beautiful Princess Fiona from a fire-breathing dragon in return for getting his swamp back. They succeed.

On the journey home, Shrek and Fiona fall in love. But the princess guards a dark secret – by night she is an ugly ogre. When she kisses her true love for the first time she will take on love's true form. Shrek and Fiona fall out, so she marries Farquaad – but just before they kiss Shrek arrives and confesses love. His kiss breaks the spell and Fiona is transformed into an ogre – her true love's form.

In *Shrek 2*, Fiona's parents struggle to accept the newly-wed ogres. To complicate matters Fiona's dad is bound by a promise he made to Fairy Godmother – that her son, Prince Charming, could marry Fiona when they grew up. Thinking Fiona would prefer him to look like a prince, Shrek drinks a magic potion that transforms both of them into beauties. But Fiona doesn't care – for them, 'happily ever after' means turning back to their ugly selves.

Key Issue: The Shrek factor

Shrek is no ordinary cartoon hero. Part of the wonderful fascination of Shrek is the discovery that he is a loveable ogre, when in traditional fairy tales the ogre is always the bad guy. Shrek wins us over just as he is. Our Bible study looks at fairy-tale endings, even when they are not what we expect, and beauty, even when that is truly in the eye of the beholder. Fiona's parents certainly see things differently in *Shrek 2*. So what about parental expectations, or the rejection Shrek endures? You don't have to be computer-animated to experience these issues, so how can the Bible help?

Bible Study

Choose one question from each section.

1   The rejection of Shrek

Lord Farquaad: [Looking at Shrek.] **What is that? It's hideous! ... Knights, new plan. The one who kills the ogre will be named champion. Have at him!** (*Shrek*)

◆   Read Isaiah 52:13 – 53:12. How did the Servant of the Lord (ie the Messiah) experience rejection? Why was this suffering 'the Lord's will' (verse 10)?

   Leaders: Note verse 2 – the Messiah did not look like a king.

◆   Read Luke 5:12–16. In what ways would this man have experienced rejection? How did Jesus reinstate him?

   Leaders: People with leprosy were social outcasts, being considered 'unclean'; healing had to be validated by the priest.

2   The beauty of Fiona

Fiona: [Expecting to be transformed from an ogre.] ***But I don't understand. I'm supposed to be beautiful!***
Shrek: ***But you are beautiful.***
Donkey: ***I was hoping this would be a happy ending.*** (*Shrek*)

◆   Read Luke 13:10–17. Contrast how Jesus and others saw this woman. In what ways did Jesus set her free?

◆   Read 1 Peter 3:1–7. What is the relationship between beauty and hope? What makes a woman beautiful?

Leaders: In 'be submissive' no inferiority of status is inferred. See 1 Peter 5:5b and Colossians 3:12–19 for how we should all be relating to one another as God's chosen people. 'Weaker partner' presumably refers to physical strength.

3   Parental expectations

Donkey: ***Oh, Shrek. Don't worry. Things just seem bad because it's dark and rainy and Fiona's father hired a sleazy hitman to whack you.*** (*Shrek 2*)

◆   Read Genesis 25:27–34; 27:1–29. In what ways did Rebekah influence Jacob? Why do you think Jacob went along with the plan?

◆   Read Ephesians 5:31 – 6:4 and Colossians 3:20,21. What tension does Paul draw out between parent and child? How do you honour parents when you're married?

4   Fairy-tale endings

Shrek: [Reading a fairy tale.] ***'She waited in the dragon's keep in the highest room in the tallest tower for her true love, and true love's first kiss.' Like that's ever gonna happen! What a load of ...*** (*Shrek*)

◆   Read Exodus 14:10–31. Trace the Israelites' spiritual journey on route to this 'fairy-tale ending'.

Leaders: The Israelite nation had just escaped from slavery in Egypt and thought they were safe. But the Egyptian Pharaoh changed his mind and decided to get them back.

◆   Read Matthew 16:13–28. Why was Peter disappointed? What perspective did Jesus have on future events?

Leaders: Jewish expectations for the coming Messiah had become dominated by a desire for a new David who would throw off the yoke of the Roman Empire – but Jesus' kingdom is not of this world (see John 18:36).

Implications

Donkey: *What's your problem, Shrek? What you got against the whole world, anyway?*
Shrek: *I'm not the problem, okay? It's the world that seems to have a problem with me. People take one look at me and go, 'Aah! Help! Run! A big, stupid, ugly ogre!' They judge me before they even know me. That's why I'm better off alone.* (Shrek)

Choose one or more of the following questions.

◆ Most of us have had Shrek-like moments when we have felt 'different' or rejected. Do you have memories which need healing? Can you offer one another help and encouragement?

◆ What is a balanced, godly response to the beauty-obsessed culture we live in?

◆ How do you relate to those the world perceives as 'ugly' in some way or another?

◆ Who are the outcasts in our society, and how can we treat them as Jesus would?

◆ What would you say to someone who doesn't believe in God because of all the things that have gone wrong in their lives?

◆ How do you deal with difficult parental expectations? If you are a parent, are there areas of your children's lives that you need to let go of?

◆ What helps you to keep believing in God's love for you when fairy-tale endings are not happening in your life?

Prayer

Spend some time praying through these issues.

Background Reading

You will find links to some background reading on the Connect Bible Studies website: www.connectbiblestudies.com

Discuss

Discuss this study in the online discussion forums at www.damaris.org/discuss/

Members' Sheet – *Shrek & Shrek 2*

Summary

Shrek is an ugly ogre who prefers a life of solitude to rejection. At the beginning of the film, he reads a fairy tale with sarcasm: 'Once upon a time there was a lovely princess ...' He has no time for fairy tales or fairy-tale creatures – until a talking donkey appears. Donkey is on the run from the evil Lord Farquaad, who has banished all fairy tale creatures from his realm and designated Shrek's swamp as their new home. Furious at the disruption, Shrek sets off with Donkey to claim it back. He strikes a deal with Farquaad – he will rescue the beautiful Princess Fiona from a fire-breathing dragon in return for getting his swamp back. They succeed.

On the journey home, Shrek and Fiona fall in love. But the princess guards a dark secret – by night she is an ugly ogre. When she kisses her true love for the first time she will take on love's true form. Shrek and Fiona fall out, so she marries Farquaad – but just before they kiss Shrek arrives and confesses love. His kiss breaks the spell and Fiona is transformed into an ogre – her true love's form.

In *Shrek 2*, Fiona's parents struggle to accept the newly-wed ogres. To complicate matters Fiona's dad is bound by a promise he made to Fairy Godmother – that her son, Prince Charming, could marry Fiona when they grew up. Thinking Fiona would prefer him to look like a prince, Shrek drinks a magic potion that transforms both of them into beauties. But Fiona doesn't care – for them, 'happily ever after' means turning back to their ugly selves.

Key Issue

Bible Study notes

Implications

Prayer